Art Smart

Spot the Details and Find Out the Facts!

Dover Publications, Inc.
Mineola, New York

How To Use This Book:

1. Look carefully at the museum wall and study the painting for 30 seconds.

2. Identify as many details as you can see about the content, colors and composition.

3. Turn the page to read ten questions about the painting from the previous page.

4. You can go back and forth to study the painting again, but try to capture as many details in your mind as possible during your first view.

5. Check the glossary at the back of the book if there are descriptive terms that you are not certain of.

6. As you look at the painting, get ready for the Big Test, which asks questions from throughout the entire museum.

7. Check your responses on the answer pages at the end of the book.

Developed by Hourglass Press LLC
Design by Coral Communications & Design LLC
Author: Sandy Chang
Design Assistants: Elizabeth Kim and Sandy Chang

Bibliographical Note
Art Smart: Spot the Details and Find Out the Facts! is a new work, first published by Dover Publications, Inc., in 2015

International Standard Book Number
ISBN-13: 978-0-486-79220-0
ISBN-10: 0-486-79220-X

Manufactured in the United States by Courier Corporation
79220X01   2015
www.doverpublications.com

Mona Lisa 1503–1517
Leonardo da Vinci

Mona Lisa

◊ Painted by Leonardo da Vinci
◊ From the Italian Renaissance
◊ Painted oil on wood panel
◊ Measures only 30 inches
  by 21 inches.
◊ You can visit it at the Musée du
  Louvre in Paris, France.

Can you remember?

1. What color are the Mona Lisa's eyes?

2. How many rings are on her fingers?

3. Does she have eyebrows?

4. Is she wearing a necklace?

5. What color is the sky in the painting?

6. What else is in the background?

7. What direction is her body facing?

8. Is her dress brown or green?

9. What is she leaning on?

10. Is her right hand above her left hand, or her left hand above her right hand?

The Biglin Brothers Racing 1873
Thomas Eakins

The Biglin Brothers Racing

◊ Painted by Thomas Eakins
◊ American painting
◊ Painted oil on canvas
◊ Measures 36 inches by 24 inches
◊ You can find this in the National Gallery of Art in Washington, DC.

What did you see?

1. Are there a lot of spectators watching the race?

2. What color is their boat and paddle?

3. How many boats and boat houses do you see?

4. Do you think that the brothers are winning the race?

5. Are there any competitors in the background?

6. What color is the water?

7. Are there any birds in the sky?

8. What season do you think it is in this painting?

9. Do you recall what the Biglin Brothers are wearing?

10. What is the weather like?

The Peaceable Kingdom 1837
Edward Hicks

The Peaceable Kingdom

◊ Painted by Edward Hicks
◊ American Folk painting
◊ Painted oil on canvas
◊ Measures 36 inches by 29 inches

How much do you recall?

1. How many native people are in the middle ground?

2. What are the men on the left doing?

3. How many animals are here?

4. Are they wild animals or domestic animals?

5. Do they look peaceful together?

6. What's in the background?

7. Do the people living among the animals look afraid?

8. What are the bears and the cow sharing in their mouth?

9. Is it a day or night time painting?

10. What is the color of the wolf in the painting?

Before the Rehearsal

◊ Created by Edgar Degas
◊ From 19th-century Impressionism
◊ Painted pastel and charcoal
  on paper
◊ Measures 19 inches by 25
  inches
◊ You can find this at the Denver
  Art Museum in Colorado.

What did it look like?

1. What are the ballerinas doing?

2. What are the two people sitting on?

3. What are the colors of the bows on the ballerinas bodies?

4. Are the two people behind the ballerinas male or female?

5. Can you recall the color of the dresses the ballerinas are wearing?

6. What is the color of the bracelet on the ballerina's hand?

7. Can we see the ballerinas' facial expressions?

8. Are the ballerinas wearing any shoes?

9. What color is the wall?

10. How many ballerinas are there in total?

Hunters in the Snow 1565
Pieter Bruegel

Hunters in the Snow

◊ Painted by Pieter Bruegel the Elder
◊ From the Renaissance
◊ Painted oil on wood panel
◊ Measures 64 inches by 46 inches
◊ You can visit this at the Kunsthistorisches Museum in Vienna, Austria

What were the details?

FACT:
This painting belongs to a series of six, but only five paintings survive. Each one shows a different time of the year.

1. What does it look like the villagers are doing?

2. Are there any leaves on the trees?

3. Does the painting have mostly cool colors or warm colors?

4. Are the hunters returning from or leaving for the hunt?

5. Are the hunters riding horses?

6. How many hunters are there?

7. What colors are the buildings?

8. Do you think the water is frozen?

9. How many hunting dogs are there?

10. Do the hunters and dogs look lively or tired?

Self-Portrait with Monkey

◊ Painted by Frida Kahlo
◊ Surrealist painting
◊ Oil on hardboard
◊ Measures 12 inches by 16 inches
◊ You can visit it at the Albright-Knox Art Gallery in Buffalo, N.Y.

What did you see?

FACT:
Frida Kahlo mostly painted self-portraits after her divorce. The portraits were made to express her mood.

1. Is she wearing anything around her neck?

2. What is holding the necklace together?

3. What animal is in the painting?

4. Does it have anything on its neck?

6. What is the color of her hair?

5. What is the expression of the animal?

7. Does she look sad, serious, or emotionless?

9. Is she making eye contact with you?

8. What can you see in the background?

10. Can you recall the color of the background?

When Will You Marry?

◊ Painted by Paul Gauguin
◊ Impressionist painting
◊ Painted oil on canvas
◊ Measures 30 inches by 40 inches
◊ You can visit it at the Kunstmuseum Basel in Switzerland.

How much do you recall?

FACT:

Gauguin left for Tahiti in 1895 and never returned to France. He stated he was escaping from "everything that is artificial and conventional."

1. How many women do you see in the foreground?

2. Are they wearing any shoes?

3. Is there any decoration in their hair?

4. Are they looking in the same direction?

5. How many people are in the background?

6. What else is in the background?

7. Can you tell what time of day it is?

8. Can you see any leaves on the tree?

9. Are they wearing any jewlery?

10. Are they wearing the same outfit?

The Bedroom 1889
Vincent van Gogh

The Bedroom

◊ Painted by Vincent van Gogh
◊ Post-impressionist painting
◊ Oil on canvas
◊ Measures 29 inches by 22 inches
◊ This painting is located at the Van Gogh Museum in Amsterdam, Netherlands.

What were the details?

1. What color is the wall?

2. How many chairs are in the room?

3. How many doors do you recall?

4. Are there any windows?

5. What color is the bed sheet?

6. How many paintings are hanging on the wall?

7. Are the paintings about the same subject?

8. How many objects are on the night stand?

9. How many clothing articles are in the painting?

10. What kind of texture did van Gogh create for the floor?

The Marriage of Giovanni Arnolfini
and Giovanna Cerami 1434
Jan van Eyck

The Marriage of Giovanni Arnolfini and Giovanna Cerami

◊ Painted by Jan van Eyck
◊ Medieval art painting
◊ Painted tempera on wood
◊ Measures 32 inches by 24 inches
◊ This painting is located at the National Gallery in London, UK

What did you see?

FACT:
You can see the artist's self-portrait and the portrait of the ceremony witness in the mirror at the background of the painting.

1. What color is the dress?

2. What pet does the couple have?

3. Is the groom wearing a hat?

4. Do you recall if the couple are holding hands?

5. What color is the furniture?

6. Do you remember if there is a window in the painting?

7. Is there any writing above the mirror?

8. What else is on the floor?

9. Can you see the bride's feet?

10. Is it an outdoor or indoor ceremony?

Henry VIII 1539–40
Hans Holbein the Younger

Henry VIII

◊ Painted by Hans Holbein the Younger
◊ From the Renaissance
◊ Painted oil on panel
◊ Measures 29 inches by 35 inches
◊ You can visit it at the National Museum of Rome, Italy.

What did it look like?

1. What is the background color of this painting?

2. Who was Henry VIII?

3. How many rings is he wearing?

4. Does he have any facial hair?

5. What does the Latin inscription mean?

6. What is Henry VIII holding in his right hand?

7. Is he wearing a hat?

8. What is the color of his hat?

9. What other decorations are on the hat?

10. What is the color of the fur?

Snap the Whip 1872
Winslow Homer

Snap the Whip

◊ Painted by Winslow Homer
◊ American painting
◊ Painted oil on canvas
◊ Measures 36 inches by 22 inches
◊ This painting belongs to a private collection.

What were the details?

1. How many kids are holding on to each other?

2. Are they wearing any shoes?

3. Are they wearing hats?

4. What is the color of the house at the back?

5. What else can you see in the background?

6. Does it seem like a nice day?

7. Are there any flowers around them?

8. Does it look like the kids are having fun?

9. What does the girl in the background have in her hand?

10. Are there any adults around?

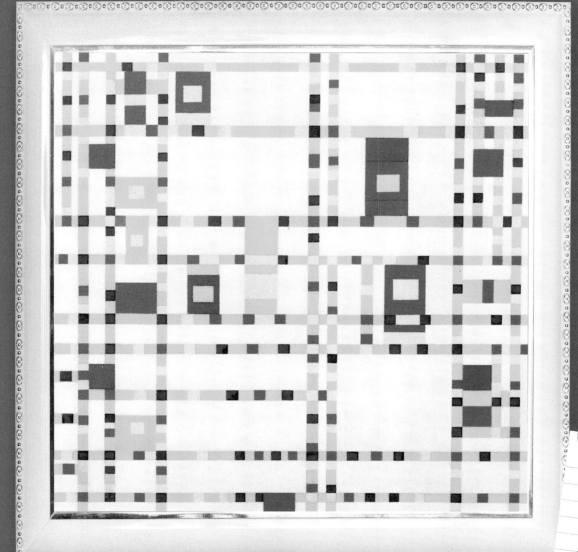

Broadway Boogie-Woogie

◊ Painted by Piet Mondrian
◊ De Stijl painting
◊ Oil on canvas
◊ Measures 50 inches by 50 inches
◊ This painting is on display at the Museum of Modern Art in New York.

How much do you recall?

1. What colors are used in the painting?

2. Does the painting look busy or calm?

4. Can you spot the artist's signature?

3. What are the shapes used in this painting?

5. Are there any secondary colors in this painting?

6. Which color is used the most?

9. What is the structure of this artwork based on?

7. Which color is used the least?

8. This painting is inspired by what kind of music?

10. Are there any diagonal lines?

Place du Théâtre Français, Rain 1898
Camille Pissarro

Place du Théâtre Français, Rain

◊ Painted by Camille Pissarro
◊ Impressionist painting
◊ Oil on canvas
◊ Measures 36 inches by 29 inches
◊ It is located at Minneapolis Institute of Arts in Minnesota.

Can you remember?

1. What is the weather like?

2. Are there any leaves on the trees?

3. What animals are pulling the carriages?

4. Does the city of Paris look busy?

5. Can you recall if there is a fountain in the painting?

6. What color are the buildings?

7. Are there any traffic lights during this time period?

8. Do you see the sun in the sky?

9. How many cars are there?

10. Is it night time?

Waterlilies 1914
Claude Monet

Waterlilies

◊ Painted by Claude Monet
◊ Impressionist painting
◊ Oil on canvas
◊ Measures 78 inches by 78 inches
◊ You can find it at the National Museum of Western Art in Tokyo, Japan

What did it look like?

1. Is the painting a cool or warm tone?

2. Are there any flowers blooming?

3. What kind of plants are in the painting?

4. Do you see any reflections of buildings in the water?

5. Is it currently raining in the painting?

6. Can you see what's underneath the water?

7. Is it during the day or night time?

8. What kind of style is this garden?

9. Around what season do you think this is?

10. What color are the flowers?

Girl with a Pearl Earring 1665–66
Jan Vermeer

Girl with a Pearl Earring

◊ Painted by Jan Vermeer
◊ Baroque painting/Dutch Golden Age
◊ Oil on canvas
◊ Measures 16 inches by 19 inches
◊ This painting is located in Mauritshuis Royal Picture Gallery in The Hague, Netherlands.

What did you see?

1. Does the subject look afraid or mysterious?

2. Who is the model?

3. What colors are her head piece?

4. What is the color of her lips?

5. What color is the background?

6. Is her shirt brown or blue?

7. Can you recall what's in the background?

8. Which way is her head turned?

9. What color are her eyes?

10. Where is the light source coming from?

The Scream 1893
Edvard Munch

The Scream

◊ Painted by Edvard Munch
◊ From the Expressionist Era
◊ Oil, tempera, and pastel on cardboard
◊ Measures 36 inches by 29 inches
◊ You can visit it at the National Gallery in Oslo, Norway.

How much do you recall?

1. Do you see any boats in the background?

2. What body of water is seen in the landscape?

3. What colors are seen in the sky in the painting?

4. Is his mouth open or closed?

5. What color are the clothes that the main subject is wearing?

6. How many people are in the painting?

7. What is the main subject leaning on?

8. What does the facial expression remind you of?

9. What shape is used the most?

10. What is the color of his face?

A Bar at the Folies-Bergère 1881–82
Édouard Manet

A Bar at the Folies-Bergère

◊ Painted by Édouard Manet
◊ Realist painting
◊ Painted oil on canvas
◊ Measures 51 inches by 38 inches
◊ This painting is at the Courtauld
  Gallery in London, UK.

What did it look like?

FACT:

The bartender's back is facing towards the mirror.

1. What is the mirror reflecting in the background?

2. What is the color of her dress?

3. Is there a chandelier hanging from the ceiling?

4. Does the bartender look happy?

5. What is the focal point of the painting?

6. Are there flowers at the bar?

7. Is the room crowded?

8. What fruit is present at the bar?

9. What is on the neck of the bartender?

10. How many bottles are on the front counter?

Luncheon of the Boating Party 1880–81
Pierre-Auguste Renoir

Luncheon of the Boating Party

◊ Painted by Pierre-Auguste Renoir
◊ Impressionist painting
◊ Oil on canvas
◊ Measure 68 inches by 51 inches
◊ You can find it at the Phillips Collection in Washington, DC.

Can you remember?

1. How many people are drinking at the moment?

2. Do they look like they are having fun?

3. What color is the awning?

4. How many people are wearing sleeveless shirts?

5. Are they on a boat?

6. Are there plants in the background?

7. What color is the dog?

8. What meal are they eating?

9. How many people are wearing hats?

10. What is the color of the table cloth?

A Sunday Afternoon on the Island
of La Grande Jatte 1884–86
Georges Seurat

A Sunday Afternoon on the Island of La Grande Jatte

◊ Painted by Georges Seurat
◊ Impressionist, pointillist painting
◊ Oil on canvas
◊ Measures 121 inches by 81 inches
◊ This painting is at the Art Institute of Chicago.

How much do you recall?

1. What activities are people doing in the park?

2. What day of the week is it?

3. Is the water on the right or left side of the painting?

4. What season do you think it is?

5. How many umbrellas are opened in the painting?

6. Who is skipping in the painting?

9. Does it look like the people are having a good time?

8. Do you remember what the weather is like?

7. What kind of animals are there?

10. Were there any boats in the background?

The Cradle

◊ Painted by Berthe Morisot
◊ Impressionist painting
◊ Oil on canvas
◊ Measures 18 inches by 22 inches
◊ It is located at the Musée d'Orsay in Paris, France.

What were the details?

1. Does the baby have a doll?

2. What is the color of the wall?

3. Can you recall what is on the mother's neck?

4. What color is the cradle's canopy?

5. Is the mother's hair tied up?

6. Can you see another family member in the painting?

7. Is the baby sleeping in the cradle?

8. What color dress is the mother wearing?

9. Who is the mother?

10. Is the baby a girl or a boy?

The Gleaners 1857
Jean-François Millet

The Gleaners

◊ Created by Jean-François Millet
◊ Realist painting
◊ Oil on canvas
◊ Measures 44 inches by 33 inches
◊ You can visit it at the Musée d'Orsay in Paris, France.

What did you see?

1. How many women are in the foreground?

2. What are the women doing?

3. What are the colors of their bandanas?

4. Do the women have baskets?

5. Can you see any people in the background?

6. What are the people in the background doing?

7. Can you see any animals in the background?

8. Is the weather good?

9. What is this painting supposed to reflect?

10. Can you see the horizon in the painting?

The Sleeping Gypsy 1897
Henri Rousseau

The Sleeping Gypsy

◊ Painted by Henri Rousseau
◊ Naïve Art
◊ Painted oil on canvas
◊ Measures 79 inches by 51 inches
◊ You can visit this painting at the Museum of Modern Art in New York.

What did it look like?

FACT:
This painting has been an inspiration for poetry and music.

1. How many stars are there?

2. What is the gypsy doing?

3. Do you remember any objects around the gypsy?

4. Can you recall what type of animal is in the painting?

5. Is there any water in the painting?

6. Is it a day or night-time painting?

7. What is the color of the mountain?

8. What is the color of her hair?

9. What is in the background?

10. Which hand of hers is holding the stick?

Las Meninas

◊ Painted by Diego Velásquez
◊ Baroque painting
◊ Oil on canvas
◊ Measures 125 inches by 109 inches
◊ You can find this at National Museum of Prado in Madrid, Spain.

What did it look like?

1. What is the color of the pet?

2. Is it a sunny day or rainy day?

3. How many people are presented in the artwork?

4. Does the princess look afraid or confident?

5. What are those things hanging on the wall?

6. What color is the princess's hair?

7. What color is the dress that the princess is wearing?

8. Was the canvas taller than everyone else?

9. Who is in the mirror?

10. What is the artist holding in the painting?

Self-Portrait at the Easel

◊ Painted by Judith Leyster
◊ Dutch Golden Age painting
◊ Oil on canvas
◊ Measures 26 inches by 30 inches
◊ You can find this painting at the National Gallery of Art in Washington, DC.

What did you see?

FACT:

Judith Leyster was one of the three important women artists during the Dutch Golden Age.

1. Who is the woman in the painting?

2. What is she leaning on?

3. Is she wearing any head piece?

4. What items is she holding in her hands?

5. Can you recall the color of her dress?

6. Is her mouth opened or closed?

7. What is the color of her hair?

8. Does she look confident?

9. What is she painting?

10. What is the color of the background?

*Still Life with a Ginger Jar
and Eggplants 1893–94*
Paul Cézanne

Still Life with a Ginger Jar and Eggplants

◊ Painted by Paul Cézanne
◊ Impressionist painting
◊ Painted oil on canvas
◊ Measures 37 inches by 29 inches
◊ This painting is at the Metropolitan Museum of Art in New York.

How much do you recall?

1. What is the subject of the painting?

2. How many bottles and vases can you count?

3. What are the colors of the tablecloths?

4. Is there any pattern on the blue cloth?

5. What are the colors of the vases?

6. How many eggplants can you count in the painting?

7. Is it a warm tone or cool tone painting?

8. How many fruits are there?

9. What is the color of the wall?

10. What is the color of the bottle?

Gazelles

◊ Painted by Franz Marc
◊ Expressionist painting
◊ Tempera on paper
◊ Measures 28 inches by 22 inches
◊ This painting belongs to a private collection.

Can you remember?

1. Is the painting mostly a warm tone or a cool tone?

2. Can you call it a true depiction of the surroundings?

3. How many gazelles are in the painting?

4. Do you see any other animal?

7. Is the painting more abstract or naturalistic?

6. What are the main colors used in this painting?

5. What shape is used the most?

8. Are the gazelles eating?

9. How many eyes are there?

10. What color are the gazelles?

The Birthday 1915
Marc Chagall

The Birthday

◊ Painted by Marc Chagall
◊ Expressionist painting
◊ Painted oil on cardboard
◊ Measures 79 inches by 51 inches
◊ This painting is at the Museum of Modern Art in New York.

What did you see?

1. Who is the couple in the painting?

2. Is the man floating in the air?

3. What is the woman holding in her hand?

4. What is the couple doing?

5. Can you recall the color of the floor?

6. What is the color of his shirt?

7. Are her eyes opened or closed?

8. What is the color of her dress?

9. How many windows can be found?

10. How many items are on top of the table?

Washington Crossing the
Delaware 1851
Emanuel Leutze

Washington Crossing
the Delaware

◊ Painted by Emanuel Leutze
◊ American painting
◊ Painted oil on canvas
◊ Measures 255 inches by 149
  inches
◊ This painting is located at the
  Metropolitan Museum of Art in
  New York.

What did it look like?

1. Which flag is shown in the painting?

2. What season could this be?

3. How are they crossing the river?

4. When was the first painting destroyed?

5. Are there any animals on the boats?

6. What can you see in the background?

7. What river are they crossing?

8. Can you see the horizon?

9. What else is in the river?

10. Who is leading the troops?

The Big Test

Use all the paintings in this book and your knowledge to answer the following questions.

1. How many female artists were there?

2. How many male artists were there?

3. Which artists painted a self-portrait?

4. Are there more female or male subjects?

5. What style of painting is present the most throughout the book?

6. How many paintings have animals in them?

7. Are there more sunny or rainy paintings?

8. How many paintings have a body of water in them?

9. Which artworks are still life paintings?

10. How many paintings have a landscape background?

11. How many paintings have paintings in them?

12. Which outdoor paintings are during winter time?

13. How many paintings have children in it?

Answer Key

p. 3

1. Brown
2. None
3. No
4. No
5. Brownish-Green
6. Mountains, roads, water & a bridge
7. Her right, our left
8. Brown
9. A chair
10. Her right hand is above her left hand

p. 13

1. Yes
2. A red thread
3. A monkey
4. Yes
5. It's emotionless
6. Black & green
7. She looks serious
8. Leaves
9. Yes
10. Blue

p. 5

1. Not that many
2. Brown & yellow
3. Six
4. Yes
5. Yes
6. Blue
7. No
8. Spring or Summer
9. T-shirts & shorts
10. It is sunny

p. 15

1. Two
2. No
3. Sunflowers
4. No
5. Two
6. Mountains, trees, & grass
7. Afternoon
8. Yes
9. Yes
10. No

p. 7

1. Five people
2. They are signing a peace treaty
3. Fourteen
4. Both
5. Yes
6. Mountains & water
7. No
8. They are sharing a branch
9. Day time
10. Gray

p. 17

1. Blue
2. Two
3. Two
4. Yes
5. Red & white
6. Six
7. No
8. Seven
9. Five
10. Wooden texture

p. 9

1. They're preparing for the rehearsal
2. A bench
3. Blue
4. Female
5. White
6. Black
7. No
8. Yes
9. Yellowish-brown
10. Two

p. 19

1. Green
2. A dog
3. Yes
4. Yes
5. Red
6. Yes
7. Yes
8. A pair of sandals & a rug
9. No
10. Indoor

p. 11

1. Working & ice-skating
2. No
3. Cool colors
4. They are returning
5. No
6. Three
7. Brown
8. Yes
9. Fourteen
10. They look tired

p. 21

1. Green
2. He was the king of England
3. Two
4. Yes, he has a beard.
5. He is 49 years old
6. A pair of brown gloves
7. Yes
8. Black
9. A feather and some jewels.
10. Brown

1. Seven
2. No
3. Yes
4. Red
5. Some people and mountains
6. Yes
7. Yes
8. Yes
9. Hoop
10. Yes, in the background

p. 23

1. A night club
2. Dark blue
3. Yes
4. No
5. The lady
6. Yes
7. Yes
8. Oranges
9. A necklace
10. Twelve

p. 35

1. Red, yellow, blues and white
2. Busy
3. Rectangles & Squares
4. No
5. No
6. Yellow
7. Blue
8. American Jazz
9. New York City map
10. No

p. 25

1. One
2. Yes
3. Orange and white stripes
4. Two
5. No
6. Yes
7. Brown
8. Lunch
9. Twelve
10. White

p. 37

1. It's a rainy day.
2. No
3. Horses
4. Yes
5. Yes
6. Beige with gray roofs
7. No
8. No
9. There are no cars
10. No

p. 27

1. Fishing, rowing boats, knitting & chatting
2. Sunday
3. Left
4. Spring or summer
5. Seven
6. A little girl
7. Dogs & a monkey
8. It's sunny
9. Yes
10. Yes

p. 39

1. Cool tone
2. Yes
3. Waterlilies
4. No
5. No
6. No
7. Day
8. Japanese-style garden
9. Spring or summer
10. Mainly purple & white

p. 29

1. No
2. Brown
3. A black necklace
4. White and pink
5. Yes
6. No
7. Yes
8. Dark blue with black stripes
9. She is the artist's sister
10. A girl

p. 41

1. She looks mysterious.
2. Vermeer's daughter
3. Blue & yellow
4. Red
5. Black
6. Brown
7. Nothing
8. Toward her left
9. Brown
10. It's coming from the upper left

p. 31

1. Three
2. Picking up the harvest
3. Pink, blue & yellow
4. No
5. Yes
6. Collecting the harvest
7. Yes
8. Yes
9. It reflects the poor people
10. Yes

p. 43

1. Yes
2. A river
3. Red, orange, yellow & some green
4. Open
5. Black
6. Three
7. A bridge
8. A man screaming
9. Circles
10. Yellow

p. 33

1. Six
2. Sleeping
3. A guitar & a vase
4. A lion
5. Yes
6. Night time
7. Gray
8. Purple & pink
9. Mountains & water
10. Her right hand

p. 45

1. Brown
2. It's a sunny day
3. Eleven
4. Confident
5. Paintings
6. Blonde
7. White
8. Yes
9. The King and the Queen
10. He is holding paint brushes and a palette

p. 47

1. Judith Leyster, the artist
2. A chair
3. Yes
4. Paint brushes, a palette & a cloth
5. Black & purple
6. Open
7. Black
8. Yes
9. A violinist
10. Gray

p. 49

1. It's a still life
2. Three
3. Blue & white
4. Yes
5. Green & blue
6. Three
7. Cool tone
8. Nine
9. Blue
10. Brown

p. 51

1. Mostly warm tone
2. No
3. Four
4. No
5. Circles
6. Red, yellow, green, blue & brown
7. Abstract
8. No
9. Five
10. Brown & yellow

p. 53

1. The artist & his wife
2. Yes
3. A bouquet of flowers
4. They are kissing
5. Red
6. Green
7. Open
8. Black
9. Two windows
10. Five

p. 55

1. American flag
2. Winter
3. On a boat
4. World War II
5. Yes
6. Mountains, river, sky & more boats
7. Delaware River
8. Yes
9. Ice
10. George Washington

p. 57

The Big Test

1. Three
2. Twenty-five
3. Diego Velásquez, Jan van Eyck, Frida Kahlo, Judith Leyster & Marc Chagall
4. Female
5. Impressionism
6. Eleven
7. There are more sunny paintings
8. Nine
9. *The Bedroom* & *Still Life With a Ginger Jar and Eggplants*
10. Ten
11. Three
12. *Washington Crossing the Delaware* & *Hunters in the Snow*
13. Six

Glossary

Abstract
A style of art that is unrealistic and has unusual lines, colors, and shapes. They usually have bold and bright colors.

Background
The part of an artwork that is the furthest distance away.

Baroque
A style of art which originated in Italy during the early 17th century, which uses strong lighting and stage-like effects to make the piece look dramatic.

Color Wheel
Colors arranged in a specific order in the shape of a circle.

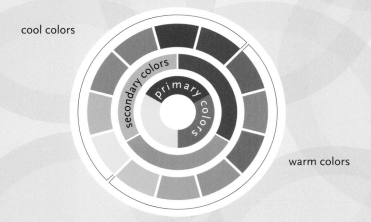

cool colors

warm colors

Complementary color
Colors that contrast with one another and are the opposing color on the color wheel.

Composition
The arrangement of the elements within an artwork.

Cool tone
This color palette includes all colors and shades of green, blue, and purple.

Cubism
A style of art which includes geometric planes and compressed space, which creates a fragmented composition.

De Stijl
A style of art which uses primary colors, rectangular shapes, and asymmetrical compositions.

Dutch Golden Age
During the 17th century, Dutch science, military, and art were among the most acclaimed in the world.

Expressionism
A style of art which uses simple designs and brilliant colors to express feelings.

Focal point
The main focus of an artwork.

Folk Art
A style of art that reflects the artist's culture or tradition.

Foreground
The part of an artwork that is the closest to the viewer.

Geometric
Rectilinear or curvilinear shapes.

Horizon
The line in which the ground and sky meet.

Impressionism
A style of art during the late 19th and early 20th centuries, which paid special attention to light.

Landscape
An artwork that shows outdoor scenery.

Light source
The point of origin where light comes from.

Medieval art
A style of art characterized by using icons and symbols to show Biblical scenes.

Middle ground
The part of an artwork that is between the foreground and the background.

Naïve art
A style of art in which the subject matter and technique has a childlike simplicity.

Organic
Shapes and forms similar to those in nature.

Pointillism
A technique of painting in which small, distinct dots of colors are applied in order to form an image.

Primary color
The primary colors are red, yellow, and blue.

Realism
A style of art in which common everyday scenes are the focus.

Renaissance
A style of art in which classical art, architecture, and literature is reborn.

Romanticism
A style of art which places emphasis on spiritual and emotional themes.

Secondary color
The secondary colors are green, purple, and orange.

Self-portrait
An artwork in which the artist portrays him or herself.

Still life
An artwork showing an arrangement of inanimate objects.

Surrealism
A style of art that uses dreams and fantasy as a subject matter.

Tempera
A type of paint that is mixed with water-soluble materials.

Warm tone
This color palette includes all colors and shades of red, orange, and yellow.